How To CRUSH it on ZOOM

Effective Speaking on the Virtual Platform

DAVID MICHAEL

Copyright © 2021 David Michael

All rights reserved.

ISBN: 979-8-73917-793-3

To

Ryan, the best son a dad could ever have.

TABLE OF CONTENTS

Acknowledgements

Introduction — 1

About the Book — 5

Section 1 — 12

Humor — 13

Embracing the Fear — 25

Less is More — 35

Edutainment — 41

Section 2 — 50

The Presentation — 53

Quick Coaching — 99

Tech Stuff — 110

Bringing It All Together — 115

Why You Need Me! — 121

ACKNOWLEDGMENTS

Writing a book is a team effort! I certainly couldn't do it alone and I want to acknowledge all the people who inspired me and helped me get this project off the ground. I want to thank My family: my mother, Betty, sisters Cassie and Suzanne and brother-in-law Rob. Thank you for always supporting me and being in my corner. My son, Ryan, who always inspires me, contributes to my ideas and is the joy of my life. My manager, David Sedelmeier, and all the great friends at our Talent Network business office including Kathleen, Linda, Megan, Emma and Hannah. Thank you to great friends Frank Murgia, Matt Wohlfarth, Mimi Lohm, John Phillips, Ron Renwick and Rick Zoltun from Zoltun Design. A very special thanks to Jennifer Garrison who helped with the compilation, arranging, and editing of the book!

INTRODUCTION

Ten years ago, I decided to put my experience down on paper to help others become better communicators from the stage. I took my years in show business, working with the best comedians of our generation, and combined it with my many years of experience coaching and consulting my clients to make them better communicators and put it all into one book: Secrets from the Greenroom: A Comedian's Inside

Techniques for Effective Speaking. Since comedians work at the highest level of public speaking, I thought it was only natural to bring these secrets to the business world where effective communication is essential. I was a young standup comic by night and a communications student at the University of Pittsburgh by day and I started using the stage experience in the classroom. And it worked! With the techniques I was perfecting at night on the stage, I was also becoming a more effective speaker during the day in the classroom. Of course this would work taking the same techniques to the corporate world! Whether a comic is telling jokes at a comedy club or a CEO is giving the state of the union speech in front of the entire company, the goal is the same: to effectively communicate your message to your given audience.

Now it is time to take those same techniques to the smaller screen, the virtual platform. Times have changed and the days of packing auditoriums and stages are over, at least for a while. Communicating over a computer is essential in our world right now. The vehicle to deliver messages may have evolved from in-person to on-screen, but the techniques are the same. I have taken my greenroom experience to the computer screen and I will teach you how to deliver your best presentation. I will teach you How to Crush it on Zoom!

I promised you the most powerful secrets to effective communication on Zoom and here they are! Although these techniques were born from the stage and still work there, it is slightly different on the virtual platform because on Zoom we lose a significant part of communication: Our live audience. I perfected and narrowed down the most powerful techniques so you can get right to the heart of communication...... virtually!

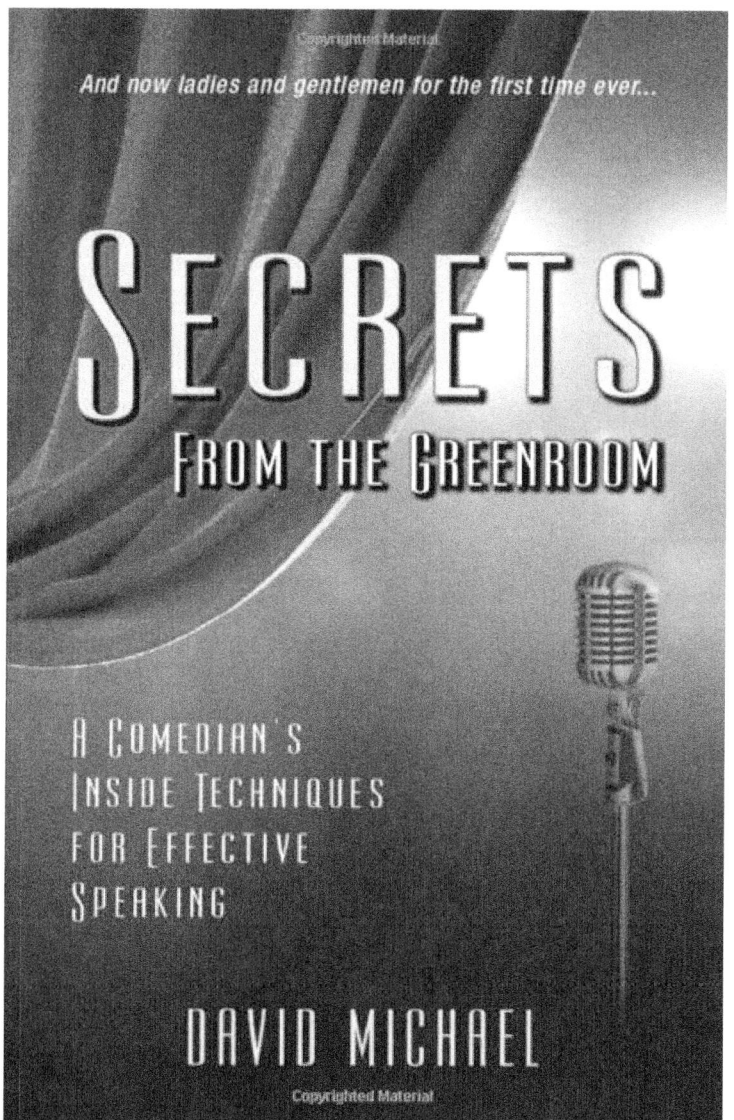

ABOUT THE BOOK

This book is different because I'm different. Too many instructional books or books by "experts" lay out a lot of "how to's" and instructions, but don't show you how to actually get it done. Well, I'm going to show you how to actually get it done...Crush It! In section one of this book, I'm going to go over my secrets with you. I'm going to lay out the three most important techniques for effectively delivering your message. I will share ideas and secrets I originated and put in my first book that still hold true today. I will introduce some new and tips to help you crush your next presentation!

In section two, I'm going to do something completely different! I am going to pull the curtain back and give you a guided tour of how to implement all those secrets and ideas and walk you through an actual presentation!! Yup. That's right folks! You'll get to see it all! I will show you how I used the techniques from section 1 and implemented those in a real presentation. We will go over what works for me and what will work for you. Remember that not everyone's the same. The idea here is to spark your creativity to find your own way of effectively delivering your message. Think of it this way: Section one is the play book and section two is the game tape that we are going to pick apart and learn from. I will give you a running commentary of the how it all comes together.

Now there are many techniques to make you a better speaker and I highlight many in my first book, but right now I'm going to focus on the three most critical techniques that you can implement right now, and it will change the way you deliver your message. These three proven techniques are the most crucial! We can never use every technique we have for a particular presentation but when I work with my clients, I always try to use the perfect combination of techniques to make sure they shine and accomplish their goal. When presenting on Zoom I came up with a combination of my techniques that will give the presenter the best success rate when using this combination.

Our philosophy and strategy in speaking in business has to change. Most businesspeople are just happy to get their information delivered without messing up and just be done! Business professionals will spend time organizing their speech and aim for perfection and this simply isn't good enough, especially on Zoom. We can't just be mistake free. We have to grab the audience's attention, keep it, and make sure they get the message. It is so much harder to communicate with your audience on Zoom and I think the biggest mistake people make is assuming that the audience is listening and giving you their undivided attention. Not so! There are too many distractions for your audience. Most people are at home and very relaxed. Too relaxed! Most are on more than one device at a time in an attempt to multitask during your very important presentation. They are answering emails and texts and only half listening to you. Some participants either don't have, or don't use their camera to be live and you are only seeing a picture or black screen. You have no idea if they are even there! I think the biggest obstacle of all is extreme screen fatigue. People are looking at screens almost 10 to 12 hours a day. We must be different and use everything we have in our arsenal to communicate our message effectively. We have to set ourselves apart from the rest of the faces and voices from the rest of the day. If we simply speak and don't get our message through to our audience, it is a complete failure. Failure! It is a harsh statement but true. When we are speaking in business our only true goal is to communicate our message, so our audience learns, retains, and acts on our performance. Using the techniques, we can focus on the effective communication before, during and after the presentation, as well as, when we are creating that presentation. It isn't enough to just deliver your presentation. You have to CRUSH it!

This book can help you consistently focus on your goal of effectively delivering your message on Zoom. From the time you create your presentation to the actual delivery you want to be consciously thinking and executing the techniques that will accomplish this goal. When speaking in business we all get caught up in just getting the message out or are just happy we didn't have any technical failures. As a speaking coach and a communications expert, I have never seen a more difficult time in my career for speaking in business. The good news is I have the most powerful techniques and anecdotes to Crush It and deliver your message effectively. All along we must remember that effective speaking is the driving force in business communication. If we fail to communicate our message everyone loses. The only reason we are there presenting…the only reason …is to effectively deliver the message.

A lot of business speaking events will still be on Zoom even though the restrictions around the world are loosening up. Now there will be a live audience and an audience on Zoom at the same time. This is called a hybrid event and will be live and live streamed and will be how many business meetings and presentations will be moving forward. This will give the participant a choice on how to attend and we need to be ready for both options. We need to be able to appeal to both audiences at the same time.

How To CRUSH it on ZOOM

SECTION 1

HUMOR

One of the best techniques to use to deliver your message is humor. As a standup comedian, I am very partial to this technique and have been using it for over 30 years. Using the same techniques, I perfected on the comedic stage and incorporating them into speeches for the business environment was the basis of my first book, "Secrets of the Greenroom". Humor transcends all audiences. Humor is memorable.

Humor is effective.

Let's talk about the importance of humor in your presentation just a bit. If you don't already know, using humor is a powerful way to communicate your message. There are studies upon studies I can list that will tell you that it is a fact that your use of humor will increase the communication and success of your presentation. Harvard, Stanford, Wharton, MIT and the London School of Business all have studies and programs on how using humor not only makes you more effective, but a strong leader as well. Stanford is now offering a class on incorporating humor in presenting and the importance and integral part humor plays in influencing your audience. They are not the only ones, but if they are that focused on it, you should be too! Look, I have been using humor to make my presentations more effective since 1985 and I can tell you as an expert you will eventually have to conform to use some type of humor in your future presentations or you will simply be left behind.

In 2013 in Las Vegas at the World Series of comedy I was asked to speak to the future comedians and leaders of communication in business and I urged them that they must absolutely use some sort of humor when they are speaking in business. According to a study by Bell Institute the 2 most desirable traits in a leader in business are work ethic and a sense of humor. If you are speaking anywhere in business you are a leader! So let's stop wasting time and start making humor a part of our presentation.

So now let's focus on why. I know and understand people don't want to, or are hesitant, to put humor in their presentation because they feel that it is not funny and it makes them uncomfortable. I hear it from my clients all the time. Well as your coach and consultant I say…get comfortable with it! Why? Because it works!! Every major speaker and company out there is using some sort of entertainment and humor in their presentations. You will be lost and left behind if you don't at least move forward and incorporate humor into yours. This is business. It's no game so you have to pull up your bootstraps and get busy. As you will see later in the book, I make it as easy as possible to slowly, and with very small adjustments, infuse humor into your presentation. If you still can't do it, you can always contact me and we will write and choreograph your presentation together. All you have to do is deliver it. That being said, you have to do this! It's really not an option anymore! So let's go!!

Ok so the value is???? OMG do I even have to tell you??? Ok, yes I will! First of all, one of the most important parts of my first book, Secrets from the Greenroom, is that as a comedian I am a natural audience expert. I have not only worked on the stage 1000s of times over the last 36 years in entertainment and business, but I have also been in the audience and observed 1000s of speakers in both businesses. I know what works and what doesn't. But the real quick answer is, everybody loves a funny speaker!! We all love to laugh, especially at business functions. We all have way too much stress and laughter relieves that!! Now more than ever since we have all been locked up with our families for over a year, we could really use humor and laughter! Haha!! Laughter also creates better bonding, team building, and it puts smiles on our faces! And the best reason of all is that it is the number one technique in effectively communicating your message to your audience. There is simply no other technique that works this well. Take it from me, when you use humor not only will they remember your message, but they will retain it as well! So when you walk off the stage or end your Zoom meeting you can drop the mic and say thank you! Goodnight! I'll be here all week!

Now I know what you're thinking. No way! I'm not

funny! I can't tell a joke! I'm not doing that! I have heard it all and I have coached so many presenters to incorporate humor into their presentations and it made all the difference. I can coach you too and I guarantee, it will make a difference!

There are so many ways to use humor in your presentation. The possibilities are endless! I'm going to give you some ideas that you can draw from, but the best idea is for you to figure out what works best for you and deliver it naturally. My intent is to get your own creative juices flowing and find a technique or idea that works for you. Everyone has a talent. Everyone is good at something. I'm trying to get you to tap into your own creativity and find what will work for you in a presentation while still making you feel comfortable and allowing you to be yourself. I do want to push you to go outside your comfort zone a little bit here, but you still have to make it work for you and most importantly, make it work for your audience.

Crush it secret one! Ok so now we know the first integral part of crushing it is humor. Since you are not a professional comedian, or a comedy writer, here is an easy way to start. When I work with my clients, we always view a video of them presenting. I want you to critique yourself as you watch your video. The easiest way to get people to get into your presentation with humor is make fun of yourself. There is no risk here. You have a lot to work with! Haha! Ok so let's go! Let's start to write some funny material about you. What do your kids say about you? Ask them. I am sure they will be more than willing to help you with this part of the presentation! How about your spouse? Or your mom or dad? What are your unique characteristics? Write these down. Put a few things together and then ask them whenever they think of something funny you do to let you know. Ask your kids to imitate you! Again, probably no shortage of material coming from them! That always stirs your creativity or gives a crushing view of how they look at you! Once you get a few things down you can start to work them into the opening of your presentation. Later in the book, in section 2, you will see how I used this exact technique in my presentation.

Telling a bad joke or failing at telling a good joke is still a good thing. It creates an endearing quality and a likability factor and the audience will pay attention too. Remember that we aren't putting on a comedy show here. We are just trying to grab the audience's attention and make them remember you and your presentation.

People are so afraid of screwing up or making a mistake that they are missing the fact that effectively communicating their message is the most important part and using your mistakes can work to your advantage. Nobody is perfect and everyone can relate to a screw up. I love mistakes!! Make fun of yourself when you make a mistake. It makes you likeable because everyone looking back at you is just happy it wasn't them and they feel for you. Use that empathy to your advantage. Now you have them right where you want them...paying attention to your message. This is a great time to insert one of your important points. If your audience is reacting to you in any way, that is what they will remember and your message will be received. I'll say it again: Messing up is not a bad thing! Not being perfect is not a bad thing! You can always turn a mistake around to work in your favor. Remember, most people are so happy that they aren't the ones speaking that they won't judge you for a mistake.

Engaging the audience is a huge weapon for you in your quest for ultimate communication of your message. As a professional comedian we always have this technique ready to go. When things aren't going our way, we can always break that 4th wall and go directly to the audience. I remember a friend years ago asked, "why do comedians always talk to people in the audience?" The answer is simple ...it works!

Now when we are talking about virtual presentations, we can still use this technique, called working the room, even though we are not in the same room. Steve Harvey taught me this great technique. When I was working on stage and people in the audience were getting distracted...like say if they were on their phones ...I would simply leave the stage while still talking and casually start approaching the person or people that were on their phones. They would always stop looking at their phones and everyone in the audience would take note. No one wants to be outed or embarrassed for not listening. When this happens, I usually deliver one of the key points I want everyone to retain and remember. I certainly know I have their attention (I'm right in the middle of the audience!) even if it is because they are so nervous that I will out someone or call on them!

Ok so how do we do this when we are on Zoom? I have a couple of different things I like to do and you can use these or develop some of your own. First, I always tell people this presentation will not be long right up front (less is more). This does two things: first in their mind, they get a little excited and relieved you will not be going on forever. You must keep your promise and definitely do not go long! People are also more intent on listening when they know you are not going to take all day. Two..I also tell them that I am going to be going to the audience during my presentation and will be asking for feedback, questions, and/or participation. This is key: in their minds they are like OMG I have to pay attention. That's right! I'm gonna be gunning for you so listen to what I say. This is just a part of knowing what your audience is all about and how they think. This sounds aggressive, but you have to keep your audience off balance to keep them in the palm of your hand.

EMBRACING THE FEAR

People do not like to give presentations...period. The main reason is fear. People are scared to death to get up in front of a group and talk. It makes them uncomfortable. What if I make a mistake? What if I freeze up? What if I forget what I am going to say? I want to relieve your stress and anxiety in speaking! I want to help you feel more comfortable when presenting your material. How can I do that you say?

Well, most of us are so concerned with nailing our presentation, and by that, I mean, not making any mistakes and hitting every one of our points that we often forget the main goal: Effectively communicating your message to your audience. When you're done, you're just so happy it's over and weeks and maybe months of anxiety is over. Well, that's great but did you effectively deliver your message, or did you just get the words out? What good did all of that research, preparation, practicing and worrying do if your audience didn't get or remember your message? If your audience wasn't listening or you didn't maintain their attention you failed. We cannot fail! Failure is not an option! Jerry Seinfeld said it best. He said the number one fear in America is public speaking. The number two fear is death. So if you're at a funeral you would be better off in the casket than you would be giving the eulogy! True ... so let's get into that and take care of it for you. It's not that serious people! Let's work on this so you are not so terrified to deliver your message.

Ok so you're putting too much pressure on yourself. Your goal isn't to not make any mistakes (remember I like mistakes! Mistakes are good!) Your goal is to effectively deliver your message. Everybody makes mistakes all the time. So what you need to do is expect them and use them to your advantage in your presentation. Yes, you can prepare for making a mistake!

As a comedian I never expect everything to go well all the time. As a matter of fact, I always expect something unusual or unexpected to happen. And you should too. If I ever get heckled, I always have several rehearsed lines I can immediately use to defuse my heckler and turn the audience to my favor. If I have a joke that bombs or doesn't do well I always have a line that I can use. These are called throw away lines and you should have some ready to go at all times. I do the same thing with mistakes. When I make a mistake, and I always do, I have at least 5 to 10 funny lines that I can use that will turn the audience my way. Most of them make fun of myself. Now I know that the idea of having to remember 5 to 10 funny lines to use on top of remembering an entire presentation seems like a lot. So work on one or two lines and use them over again if you need to. Or, as you will see in Quick Coaching, you can have a couple of lines on your cue cards ready to use at any time. No one ever expects you to be perfect and when you make a mistake a funny line or prepared line about the mistake itself will show that not only are you humble and have a sense of humor but will show the audience you are great under fire and pressure thus turning the audience into fans of yours. Think of all those times you were in an argument and couldn't think of a great comeback until hours later. This is like that. Prepare for that moment and be ready with the zinger! Most will think, "WOW! Can you believe that happened and look how they handled it!" They will think you just thought of that line even though you had it ready to go in your arsenal! Wow what a leader! If you practice this and have a couple of lines ready to go for any mistake it is also going to help you out mentally with your presentation. All the stress of messing up goes out the window. Why?! Because now you got it covered! Now even making that dreaded mistake won't mess with your psyche or throw you off your game. So having lines prepared for every situation will allow you to have the confidence to know whatever happens, you got it covered which lessens your anxiety that something bad may happen. So if you freeze up, forget what you are going to say, your cue cards fall all over your demo props, your cat runs through, your kids walk through, or someone walks behind you without pants on, you have it covered! And if you didn't have it covered just laugh and say, "You know what? I wasn't expecting that!" or "That's not something you see every day!" No problem and no anxiety! Bring it on!

Let me give you an actual example of what could go wrong and how we can plan for it. I had a client one time who worried about every little detail when he had a presentation. I had just started working with him and was observing a live presentation at a corporate function. As I sat in the audience the MC who introduced him completely screwed up his introduction. I have been in show business for a long time and have seen all kinds of really bad intros. I didn't think it was that big of a deal but to my client it was devastating. He is an expert in his field and I thought his intro was too long but he had almost every accomplishment in his career there. Out of an entire paragraph the emcee only got two things right. Now my client was expecting to get a huge bump from his introduction and now he felt slighted and that he was in a huge hole. He got in his own head and couldn't dig out. His mind really started to work against him. Needless to say, the nerves and wild imagination just completely incapacitated him from any kind of successful recovery. I felt for my client. I have been there so many times the past 30+ years. When he got off the stage he said to me I had a horrible presentation because the mc screwed up my intro. I immediately corrected him and said no you had a bad presentation because you were not correctly prepared. You let something simple rattle you instead of brushing it off, making fun of yourself and moving on to delivering that important message to your audience. I must say this here for anyone who is reading the book. If you have or can be thrown off by a bad introduction you are not preparing correctly. I must also say that all an introduction does is get you on stage. After that, it's all up to you! This is a very important lesson to learn: rolling with the punches. Use mistakes to your advantage. Are you sensing a theme here? Make fun of yourself. Make a funny face. Use anything you can to draw attention away from the mistake and make it funny. Be ready to handle anything. Prepare so well that nothing rattles you. These are very important techniques that comedians use to handle any and now you can too.

Sometimes a long introduction with too many credits sets you up to fail. So just try to keep the credits to a minimum. If your introduction is that important, and a lot of times it absolutely is, then you need to be prepared for the first intro every time.

So let's take a look at a way we can negate a bad introduction. First of all if I was in this situation I would pause when I got to the stage and say,

> "Ladies and gentlemen! I am not your speaker.....but I did stay in a Holiday Inn Express last night!"

I would then say I am only here for the introduction and then go into your intro just as you wanted it done (because nobody will introduce you the way you will)! After you introduce your name leave the stage and then reenter the stage with a quip like, "well you know folks it's tough to be the successful identical twin!" You can then look up at the sky and say, "Yes mom I know I promised!" This breaks the ice and you have a little fun with the audience and complete your goal of having your introduction done the way you need it done!

So what did we learn? Mistakes can be your friend. Use humor to get yourself out of any mistake, or pause, or lapse or distraction. Humor is your best weapon so use it. Now you've gone from being afraid of it to making it your best friend! Practice humor. Embrace humor. Use humor!!! I think you got it

LESS IS MORE

Technique number two: Less is more. I have always been a fan of less is more. I just want to give you what you need to make the small adjustments to be the most effective. My first book takes about an hour to read and is only about a hundred pages for a reason. I don't want you to get lost in too many ideas at once. I want to deliver your information to you in short, quick sections so you can absorb and retain the information. The same goes for this book. We follow the same plan. It's also how I coach. Quick, powerful techniques with just small adjustments that will make you the most effective speaker and get immediate results!

In the corporate world it has always been, let's give them all the information they could possibly handle and then some! Pull out every chart and graph and picture and load the audience up with all the statistics you can find. That will make you seem really important and convince the audience you know everything about your topic. It is still a hard mindset to break for business leaders and the corporate world as a whole. It is that mindset I want to break or reset for you! When you are presenting, or more importantly, creating your presentation it is important to limit what you are going to say into 3 main points. Or one major point and two minor points. I know you have an avalanche of information you need them to know but a presentation is not the time to go into all of it. First of all, your audience today cannot and simply will not absorb all the information you deliver. And when you just simply start stating facts and numbers for any length of time the audience is gone. So you have missed the mark and failed!

Now I know we still need to get the information to them so let's try it like this. Make your presentation as fun as you possibly can by using humor and edutainment (sneak peek!) so your audience will enjoy you and your material. After you have crushed it in your presentation, you can always direct them to a document or invite them to a second meeting to go over details or present more information. A website, a handout you can email them, your book etc. are all great follow ups to your memorable presentation. They will be more likely to follow up, but the really important part is they effectively received your message and they will retain it! Yes! Goal achieved!

So why did I address the attention span of audiences in my last book 10 years ago? Because it was a big problem then and it is a bigger problem now! Since then, things have accelerated and now it seems that audiences have little attention or time for information being delivered virtually. The main reason? We look at screens at least 10 to 12 hours a day! That's a lot of time to be looking at a screen. Many of us have multiple gadgets going at once; phones, TVs, computers and it drains our attention. This is why it is so critical to start communicating your message quickly and effectively to grab your audience's attention. By shortening your message and adding color, humor and edutainment you give your audience a tried-and-true combination of techniques to powerfully deliver your message.

Remember this: Ted X is the most effective business speaking venture of all time. Traditionally, they only wanted speakers to present a maximum of 18 minutes. This would give the speaker enough time to get a good idea out and effectively delivered and it would give the audience a short enough presentation to keep their attention. A win-win situation. The speakers were distraught because limiting their time from 45 minutes to 18 minutes was difficult for them. But it taught them to really think about what their most important message really was. Since then, speakers have been going shorter and shorter and shorter. I just googled TedX and found several presentations that were 3 to 5 minutes long. That's right! 3 to 5 minutes! So Ted knows best….less is more…let's Crush it on Zoom!

As we stated, one of our biggest challenges today when speaking virtually is screen fatigue. Because of the pandemic people are using their screens up to 12 hours a day. That's a lot of screen time! Starting early in the morning with phones and tv and then work at the computer and finally a zoom presentation so it's conceivable that if you have a presentation in the afternoon your audience would have been looking at screens for almost 8 to 10 hours. So what are you going to do to capture and keep their attention and deliver your message? These techniques will help you effectively do that! You have to be different, and you have to stand out. Less is More.

EDUTAINMENT

Well, here we are! The most important and enlightening secret I can share with you and I even let it slip a couple of times in previous chapters because it's just that important...edutainment! It combines everything we are talking about in this book. Edutainment is combining education and entertainment. It is literally how almost all of your audience members were conditioned to learn. It is one of the most effective teaching tools of all time and can be found in all forms of learning. So now, knowing this about your audience, all you have to do is appeal to this in your presentation to be more effective! Let's take a look at what I wrote about it in my book 10 years ago.

> *There is nothing like the feeling you get from making a groupof people laugh. I remember the first time I was able to get laughs on stage as a comedian. It was one of the most exhilarating experiences of my life. As time went on, it didn't matter ifI was in a smoke-filled bar or a fancy concert hall, the feeling wasthe same. You get a sense of love and adulation, but it's the power you feel you have over the audience that's intoxicating. Once you have their trust, you can try out new material and even push*
>
> *The same is true for all speakers. If you can be entertaining, the   chances of reaching your audience are infinitely better.*
>
> *There's actually a word for this: edutainment. Obviously, it's the combination of education and entertainment. When I first heard this term I thought, "Hey, I've been doing this for years." Edutainment is becoming more pervasive in the educational world, but little has been done regarding presentationsand speech making. Nevertheless, it's predicted that an entire industry will develop around edutainment.*

That's a big deal. As more and more educators use edutainment in their classrooms their students will become conditioned to learn that way. As these students grow older they will also expect future learning experiences to be edutainment-based. If you are not entertaining while you are trying to get your subject matter across to your audience, they may not listen to your words.

The mix of educating, entertaining and humor has been a part of learning for some time; you probably didn't even realize it. I can remember back to my youth and it still resonates with me 30 years later. Now the subject matter wasn't something thatI was particularly interested in, but the message was packaged in such a way that the information still rattles around in my head. I'm talking about Schoolhouse Rock!

When people hear the words "conjunction junction what's your function?" or "I'm just a bill" they immediately recall Saturday morning cartoon images and those catchy songs that have never left them. Do you think it's a coincidence that the man responsible for the Schoolhouse Rock! *concept came from advertising? When you are teaching or presenting at a seminar or anytime you're in front of an audience you want them to remember your message.* Schoolhouse Rock! *first aired in the 1970's and there's a whole generation that can recite the lyrics to those animations thirty years later. That's pretty powerful.*

*Many of the TV programs geared toward children—*Sesame Street, Electric Company, The Muppet Show, *and the shows of today like* Super Why, Word World, Sid the Science Kid—*combine entertainment and education. The Muppet Show is* *particularly endearing to me because of Fozzie Bear, the character that wants to be a comedian. Many times during my career I've seen two old guys in the audience and immediately had visions of the two old guys that heckle Fozzie. I usually tell them they remind me of the guys from* The Muppet Show *and that gets a lot of laughs. This goes to show you the popularity of these shows and how a rehearsed "improvisational" line can work.*

The latest generation of audiences has been conditioned to learn a different way because of television. They are used to getting their information packaged in the form of entertainment. I believe this is the most important aspect of an audience that a speaker can be aware of. If you want to be an effective speaker, you must accept this fact and add edutainment to your presentation. Crowds today have grown up with Schoolhouse Rock!, *twenty-four-hour comedy networks,* YouTube, *and funny ads that people talk about over the water cooler. Kids do their homework while listening to their iPod. They expect a little spice. Give it to them, whether it's a joke, a prop, music, or even a little magic. It's all edutainment.*

Wow! How about that? We were on to something all those years ago! Since then, the edutainment industry continues to grow and become ever present in all forms of education and training. Not only are kids continuing to learn in this fashion but colleges and universities, as well. Even the corporate and tech worlds have used edutainment as an important tool to encourage innovation, new ideas, and moving the world forward. So if you are presenting and speaking today you have no choice but to infuse this powerful secret into your presentation. I know it may not be what you're used to, but let's have fun with it! Remember it's just small adjustments that will eventually lead to a big change and make a great impact. The great thing about edutainment, like humor, is that there are endless ideas and options for you. You can use props, videos, magic, humor, songs and music, sound effects, costumes, funny pictures and so on! It has never been easier to add this to your message!

How many of you ever watched Sesame Street or Electric Company or Dora the Explorer or Little Einstein's? The list goes on. What do they all have in common? They are all educational television shows, and they are designed to deliver content to children in a very specific way. It is education in a very entertaining way. These shows are designed to hold your attention with catchy tunes or phrases, bright colors and very energetic cast members. How else can you get a three-year-old to sit and watch Kermit the Frog for an hour or sing along with Dora for 30 minutes? These shows are fun and entertaining and teach you a message and most of the time, we don't even realize it. How about School House Rock?! How many of you can sing the words to Conjunction junction, What's your Function? Or, I'm Only a Bill? Did you even realize that you really learned something from these songs, or did you just sing along because it was a catchy tune? Did you find yourself singing the song in your head in English class to get the right answer? I bet you did. Well, there ya go! These programs entertain and educate at the same time. This is how we are conditioned to learn, and it started very early in our lives. Understanding how your audience wants to receive information and understanding how they will retain and enjoy that information is the key to delivering your information effectively.

We all know how this works, even if we didn't know why. How many of us will sit through a boring or fact filled tv show or presentation? We get tired and we get bored and we tune it out. But if the show has music and lots of bright colors and characters that we can relate to, just like the children's shows, we pay attention. We are entertained and we watch. If we also happen to learn that a pygmy marmoset is the smallest mammal in the world or we can speak several words in Spanish while watching, then that's a plus! It also illustrates how effective edutainment is. We learn information without trying. As speakers we have to use this to our advantage and insert these techniques into our presentation. Like humor, you don't have to be perfect at this technique. It's in the attempt that makes it effective.

What if I told you I can tell you how your audience was conditioned to learn and how they wanted you to deliver your information to them? Wouldn't that allow you to structure and deliver one of the most memorable and impactful presentations, not to mention your most important goal of effectively communicating your message to them? It's like having the answers to the test while you're studying. You know exactly what you need to know and what you need to focus on to achieve your end result. It's one of the trademark goals in the entertainment field: always give the audience what they want! In business we can use this powerful secret to CRUSH IT when we present and attain ultimate success!

Ok so here it is your actual game plan for crushing it on Zoom. We are going to show you how to structure your presentation, where to put the humor and edutainment and how to cut down on how long you are speaking. We are going to inspire you to plan for when things go wrong and always have a backup plan. We delve into what your audience wants and how you need to deliver it to them. And we keep it short, too! We only give you what you need to succeed and cut out all the BS! So here it is let's go!

SECTION 2

Okay, so remember this is exactly how I delivered the presentation, so it reads how I talk. You can see I am more of a conversationalist when I present than I am a reader of facts. This comes from being a speaker and comedian for many years. I've included some pics and notes from the presentation to give the inside secrets to what my intentions and goals were with this particular audience and point out my mistakes and how I used them to help me. I always specifically prepare my presentation to the audience I am working for, so I always include the company and a personal touch. I realize that if you viewed this presentation, you could receive the full effect including my facial expressions and goofy gestures but the real goal here is to show you how to compose and structure your presentation using these techniques for our ultimate goal of effectively communicating our message. So here we go!

THE PRESENTATION

How's everybody doing today? I hope you guys are doing good today. My name is David Michael and I am a professional comedian but I am also a communications expert and I help people in business become more effective speakers. So that's what I do. But first off today, I just want to say that this is going to be fun. I want you to relax. I want you to smile a little bit. I want you to enjoy this. The only thing I really want you to do is get your creative juices flowing because I want you to start thinking a little bit outside the box on how you can improve on the connection on Zoom because it is very difficult these days. Now I know you have a comedian on here and you're probably wondering what's he gonna do? Does he get out mellons and crush them with a big mallet? No. That's not me, that's someone else. That's not what I do.

We're going to do things a little different. Some things that are fun and some things I think you'll enjoy. I want you to start thinking in a certain way and we're going to start thinking about where the audience is coming from when they see your presentation in business.

It's really difficult at this time and I always try to start out with some of the bad news. The bad news for us today is that I haven't seen a more difficult time to effectively deliver your message in business. It really is! I think the last time it got tough, and it's not as difficult as it is now, but ten years ago maybe fifteen years ago when everyone in the audience at a live presentation would pull out their phones and start working on it. But then you could actually do something about it. You could leave the stage and start walking toward them and when they see you they can put their phone back in their pocket and everyone in the audience is going, "Oh my! I don't want that to happen to me!" and they put their phone down. So then they will actually listen to you. But the key point is we need to effectively deliver our message. So how are we going to do that?

It's even more difficult now. Now everyone is on Zoom and Zoom is kind of difficult thing because people get WAY TOO RELAXED! Right? We've seen all the videos, haven't we? Some guys are not wearing pants. Some guy's just in his underwear. You know, there's cats in the background. There's kids coming in. That's a lot of distractions. You know, so what are we going to do? We're have to gonna have to combat this some way. And the other thing we have going against us is VIDEO FATIGUE! Especially in this past year, people are on their screens all day long. Starting at six o'clock in the morning you're on your phone. You're watching TV. You go to work or if you work from home and you're on your computer. It's 2 o'clock now, or 2:05 right now so I have to take into account that you literally have been on your screens for almost 8 hours. That's a lot!! It's a lot to overcome, but you know what? We can do it! And we can do it today!

I give you a little bit of the back story. I started off in communication classes at the University of Pittsburgh years ago, but at night I was a stand-up comedian because I loved it! I just thought it was great because when you're on stage as a comedian, you're the writer, actor, director, producer, you get to do everything and

I love that creative control! But what I started to do was learn all these techniques being a stand-up comedian and I thought they were really cool, but at Pitt when I went to school I had all these communication classes. A lot of speech classes and stuff like that and I thought, boy, I have this great idea. I had this one professor who said you can talk about anything you want to talk about and you can do anything you want to do. And I thought, well that's great! Creative control! The first thing I did was…because back then, and I'm sure a lot of you remember if you're as old as I am, back then everyone spoke behind a podium. There would be a podium and then there would be a microphone there so if you were really tall the microphone would be too short and you'd have to lean over and it would be really hard to adjust. If you were too short you'd just see a head and the microphone would be way up there. I just moved the podium! I just said, you know what? I'm gonna just get rid of the podium. It's covering most of me anyways and I just want to be out here and I want to talk to you. And I remember the professor looked at me and said why did you do that? And I said because I want to relate to these people. I want to be almost touching them, not that you want to, but you want to be out there so they can see you and almost feel you, right? When you're behind a podium not that many people are paying attention. We had people falling asleep and I wanted to make sure that wasn't going to happen when I was giving my presentation.

That's where it starts for me! Then I went on the road, but before I went on the road, I had to tell my parents that instead of being a lawyer like my dad, or a teacher like my mom, I wanted to be a stand-up comedian. And they were really excited and happy for me!!! No. No they weren't!! They weren't happy at all! They were mortified that I wanted to be a comedian.

Back in the mid 80's when I went to college it wasn't

like something you wanted to do, but fortunately for me it worked out pretty well, but I just remember that I'm sure there were a lot of closed door meetings at the time and my mom and dad were talking. I think they called the hospital, you know, to see if there was some kind of mix up twenty years ago before. They really weren't, you know, fired up about it. I mean, we got beyond that and I think they're proud of me now. It's just when I look back on it now, how long I've been doing this, it's been a long, long time.

I have a son now and he's beautiful and I get these emails now that are so tech involved. The emails I used to be great, but now they are so age related like I started getting emails from AARP when I was 45! Like give me a break here! I'm not retired yet. I don't want to be. But you get all kinds of emails. I get emails now like, "are you ready for the walk in the tub?" NO! I'm not ready for that! They're like, Terry Bradshaw has one…still no..no!! Other emails I get are like, Are you planning your funeral? No! What do they know that I don't!?

My son is just a beautiful kid, but I don't think he understands what it's like to get older. Because I'm bald now and that just resonates with him. You know when you get older and you lose your hair, that's how people identify you as the bald guy. The bald guy, you know?! I was watching him on the basketball court the other day and I was watching him and one of the other kids was asking him, where's your dad and he's like, he's up there. See that bald guy right there? That's him! So…you get identified like that. It was just a wonderful thing. I think he tried to make up for it the other day. He says to me, Dad, you know who you look like? I'm all excited because maybe he's going to say The Rock or Jason Strathum or Bruce Willis or something like that. But no. No. No. He says, You look like the eagle from the Muppets!" What? The Muppets? I look like a Muppet?

Anyway, you're probably wondering what I'm doing now. This is what I usually do in my presentations. I was just doing a little standup comedy for you, making fun of myself. I want everyone to relax and I want you to have a good time and get you involved in ME, a little bit about me before I deliver my topic. And that's one of the things we're going to learn today, it's just really important to be humble, show you a little humility and be funny if you can and make fun of yourself. It's just one of those things that will really engage the audience a little bit better because we're on screen and it's really difficult. You know we're taking the live aspect away from it, it's really difficult. I know there are people right now listening to me talk and their phones and they're doing their banking. I know that! I know that! So I'm going to have to get their attention some way. You know maybe I'll get a cow bell and I'll start dinging it whenever I see that happen, right? Now I'm not going to get a cowbell, but because I said that you can imagine a cowbell dinging and that says something to you, right? Either the Will Ferrell skit or you can imagine the sound. That's what I want you to think, right? That's what I want you to think.

Okay, so here is the opening and I have a few different things going on here but you can see it is a very relaxed beginning. You can see I have a very conversational style and a warm presence. I like to let the audience know upfront what to expect and stress that we are going to have fun, smile and enjoy ourselves. This is very important as an audience expert I can tell you if you start of telling people this won't be long and we are going to have fun they will invest attention into your presentation right off the bat. Every audience wants your presentation to be fun ....not dismal.

You can also see I also give them the bad news upfront and immediately make light of it as I have the solution. Making fun of our problem lessens the severity and dread of it. Did you ever have a problem that you thought was so big and you stressed over it and dreaded what was going to happen? And then you talked to someone for help and they immediately had a viable solution! Remember how good that felt? That's all I'm doing here . Effective communication on zoom is a huge problem today but I have the solution. Now my audience is relieved and excited at the same time and I set the stage so we can have some fun too!

Remember fun! At the same time I create my expectations of what I want them doing as my presentation moves along. I want them to use my presentation to get their creative juices flowing and start getting ideas on what they can do in their own presentations. So really what we are doing is setting you the speaker up for success from the get go. As you can see I use my lighthearted low risk humorous material about myself to get my audience interested in me before I deliver my message. If your audience likes your demeanor, they will ride with you through your presentation!

So, as I look back, it was such a great ride being a standup comedian. I loved it, ya know, I did a lot of corporate parties, I worked with a lot of famous people. You know, Jay Leno, Dennis Miller and all kinds of people. It was just so exciting to be inside the greenroom when you have famous people like that. Like Ray Romano and Lewis Black and I always thought when I was in the greenroom all kinds of crazy stuff would happen, but really what would happen and what most comedians talked about in the greenroom was the audience. That's what we talked about most of the time! And I realized when we were talking about it that we have some of the most powerful techniques that you can use on the audience. And I thought, hmmm this is interesting. I wonder if this would work in the corporate market. And it does. So when I released my book, what I did was I made it from the audience's perspective. What does the audience want to see? What does the audience say? I remember

Chris Rock, when I met him for the first time, he shook my hand and asked what the audience liked tonight. And you have several different ways to describe it. You know they're either good, they're high, they're low, It's a Friday night second show audience. It's a Saturday night first show audience, all kinds of ways to describe them. And then when a comedian would hear that before he went on stage, he would start developing what bits he was going to do , how he was going to connect with that audience and how he was going to be successful. So I took those and I put them in this book right here (shameless plug here), by the way everyone gets a free copy of the book if you want. But I put a collection in here of the book so we can effectively deliver our message which is so important right now. Some of them are really some of the most powerful techniques and I make the book short. It's only 100 pages but hopefully like today it will give you some ideas on how you can increase the engagement with your audience by using these powerful techniques, cause they're really powerful and we're going to go through a couple of them right here.

It was different, it was so different, it was never any other books out there and the reason I wrote it is I didn't see any books that focused on the audience. I saw a lot of books that focused on the speaker. You know, how to stand like this. If you stand like this it means this. If you stand like this it means this. If you stand like this it means that. Well I was looking at thousands of presentations at the time in business and I never thought that when I saw people stand like that. I didn't think when a guy stands like this, I didn't think oh he's a Spartan. I didn't think that. I didn't think that at all! I was too worried about what he was saying or what they were saying and engaging, you know. And when you're funny that's the best thing you can possibly be. I think you can really engage your audience by just doing humor alone. Now we're going to learn a little bit more than humor, but when I saw it, I think it was the book that was called Public Speaking for Dummies. It's 300 pages long!! I actually read it! Not that I'm a dummy, well I might be I don't know. You can make your mind up on that. But it was 300 pages long and I was like what dummy can read 300 pages and actually use the actual 15 pages he needs or she needs for the presentation. You know it's very, very difficult so you have to find some way to get humor into your presentation.

Okay, so I'm going to drink some water here and I already know what your concerns are. I already know what you're thinking. I've heard it from my clients over the years and I know what you're thinking. You're thinking, Dave, I'm not doing it! Cause that's usually what they say. I'm not putting humor in my presentation. I'm not going to do it at all! So what are your concerns? Well I know the number one concern is people don't like to speak. And I understand that but in business we have to. We have to find a way to connect with our audience, not just speak.

I had a client one time, it was like five minutes before he was supposed to go on stage and I was there for moral support and help him out before and after and he was gone. Like I didn't see him, like 30 seconds he came back and he sat down. I'm like where were you starting in like 30 seconds. He goes I was in the bathroom. I just threw up. I feel better right now. You can't throw up before you present! It's not that serious!! Okay! You have to try to enjoy the process a little bit. I get it! I think Seinfeld said it the best. Seinfeld said the number one fear is public speaking and the number two fear is death. So at a funeral you'd be better off being in the casket than you would be giving the eulogy!! And I completely understand that. I understand that people get so…the anxiety! I got a presentation next week and then the count down and then the day of and people get so crazy with it. There's a lot of different ways we can do just for that fear. Now I'm telling you that along with that fear you also have to add a little bit of humor and some other things. I know you don't want to do it, but we have to because in business I can tell you right now the trend is all more entertainment in presentations and especially now. Zoom is not going away anytime soon. One, it's too effective, okay. Two it's too cheap. You know and it's really convenient so it's not going to go away completely I mean obviously we're going to open pretty up soon and people are going to have live meetings, but it's very convenient so we have to learn to effectively communicate our message on this platform. And if we don't then we're going to fail. We're going to fail that's it and we don't want to fail. We want to be successful. Right? Because if you're successful at effectively presenting your idea in business right/ more success more money everybody's happy.

Okay so now let's talk a little bit about risk. Because I

know when I say I need you to add humor to your presentation you're like no. I'm not going to do it. I'm not going to do it. I don't want to offend anybody. I hear that a lot. I say well that's okay. We're not going to make fun of anybody, but you. And they're like, what, me? You know, just like I did up front. Just like I did up front! Make fun of yourself. I make fun of me all the time and I don't really care. As long as you make fun of yourself everything's' going to be okay. People are going to relate to that. Oh I have the same problems as him. Oh he's goofy and I don't have those kinds of problems. I don't have a walk in tub.so. but you have to make fun of yourself..

The other things people always tell me, what if it doesn't work? What if it doesn't work? What if it doesn't work? So it doesn't work. Things don't work all the time. But let me tell you this. Failed humor is almost just as good or even better sometimes than successful humor. And people will ask me, oh Dave, you gotta be kidding me. No! It's the absolute truth! Because just like when I'm talking and I pull out that cowbell and I go like that you already know what I'm thinking, you already know the sound of the cowbell you're already thinking about something so I say something really important after it and you get it.

Let me give you, because I had a lot of bad shows in my life and I had a lot of bad presentations years ago and I always try to make sure it doesn't happen, but it does. Like when I started doing stand up comedy, there were people actually still bringing tomatoes to shows to throw at ya. Now I never had anybody throw a tomato at me. They did throw a bottle of ketchup one time. They missed thank goodness. You know what I mean!? But people always say, but what if it doesn't work. Well let me tell you one of my worst stories that I had in one of my presentations. I was hired to work at a college and I had a specific topic and the topic was getting the faculty and the students to work better together. Nice topic, but they had this great idea. Why don't we, since you're a comedian, there's going to be a faculty and student basketball game and they're going to play each other and we're going to put you on at half time at mid court. That's the worst idea I think I've ever heard in my life. I don't want any parts of it. But I did it. And I did it because I wanted to get the message to them. And I got out there and I knew it was a bad idea. You don't ever want to work in a gym when you're a comedian. You never want to work at center court at half time. It just doesn't work. So I got there and I got to center court and I started delivering my message and three minutes in absolutely nobody is listening. And I'm like ugh, this is going to be upsetting it's not going to work. So I try to do some humor, just like I did up front and every time I finished a punchline some kid that was running the clock, you know the clock that goes AHHHH like that. That little bugger every time I finished, and I paused he went EHHHHHH and I'm like I'm going to kill this kid. I am going to just wait till I get my hands on him and I was so upset, but everybody laughed. Everybody laughed!! Okay. I'm the butt of the joke. So I have to remember what my position is here. I have to effectively communicate my message. So what I decided to do is okay, these are the key points that I want to make. I'll tell you what I'm going to do. I'm going to start making these key points and then as soon as I pause, he's going to ring that buzzer. So I made my key points EHHHHH, everybody laughed. I knew they were listening to what I was saying. Not only listening but retaining that message which is so important. Remember, cow bell, right? The EHHHHH you gotta remember that. It got to a point that I just started pointing at him and EHHHHH and everybody enjoyed it.

Get the idea?

So some things don't work out. You have to try to make the best of it. You just have to try to make the best of it.

Okay, here's your last objection. I think it may be the last objection. You're going to go, Dave....I'm not funny. ☹ Well, that's okay! It's not easy being funny. Look, I'm not here today to show you how to become a comedian. I can't do that. It takes a long time. I want you to be just a little more humorous, you know, and find a way to get it in there.

One of the ways I think is the easiest way for people to get humor into their presentations, and today we're talking about the 7-minute presentation, one of the ways I find is the most effective way is if you see a comedian on tv, just mention their joke. I'm not telling you to steal material from comedians, but always mention their name and give them credit. You know I have a funny comedian I follow all the time. Her name is Sonia King, mention their name, and she has a really funny joke and I would just if I were you is just open up and say, You know I saw this really funny comedian last night, her name is Sonia King and she was talking about her dogs and she buys them the Beggin Strips and everything like that and I noticed the advertising on Beggin Strips is pretty funny. She goes Beggin Strips, because dogs don't know it's not real bacon. And then she said, well neither do my in-laws!! So it's a nice, cute way just to open up and you don't have to be funny and you don't have to write the comedy and it's really risk free, right? It's not your joke. You didn't write it. You happen to think it was funny, but it's a nice way to get in there. Because I'm telling you, with just small adjustments like that in your presentation it will go a lot further in effectively communicating your message. Just small adjustments. Okay you don't have to go overboard. We don't have to go overboard. Just small adjustments.

Let me give you an example of somebody I saw, actually it was about three weeks ago here at NaVoba, one of the veteran businesses giving a presentation. This guy was kind of funny. And I don't think he meant to be, but it was great how he did it. He had, essentially, the same information as somebody two presenters before him, but the guy two presenters before him that had the same information as him got cut off. So when he got up there, they said are you ready to go and he says yeah I'm ready to go. And he goes, this is kind of a blessing, I have kind of the same information as the other guy, he got cut off. I thought woaw, and I started listening to him. And I said well that's kind of humble and just saying what a blessing it is for him that he got it. He also did something else a little later in the presentation. And when I was listening to him and I was taking my notes like I always do, he was talking about his charts and he was talking about his graphs and he said. You know what? I did it this way cause it's a little sexier. Now obviously he was using sexier as not a term of sex, but he was using the term to make it more appealing but that word just kind of rung a bell and I looked at him and I was like, I like that word and I liked what he did so those two small adjustments, right, we're just making small adjustments to make it more effective, it made it more effective for me because I listened to him a little bit more because of that and that is the ultimate objective here.

So in closing with humor remember it's the great connector. We have to find a way to get it in there. We have to! Remember this: 10 to 12 hours a day!! That's a lot of video fatigue. How are we going to be different? How are we going to be different? I urge you to find some way to get humor in, not just for these seven-minute presentations, but moving forward in your business. You know, you're a leader. Stanford has a whole program in their leadership program teaching humor because they think it's that important. And I can tell you by being in the business, it absolutely is!!! So, I think you should, anytime you can, just try to get it in there, okay? I would give you all the information I can now, but I'm talking too long about this subject, but it's that important. It's that important to somehow get some kind of humor in there.

LESS IS MORE

Now let's talk a little bit about Less Is More.

We have a seven-minute presentation and I know when you see less is more you're obviously thinking, "Oh my God! I've got to get everything into seven minutes! I've got to get all my business, all my charts, all my graphs. I've got to get it all into seven minutes!" No! No, we don't! We have to think differently about this seven minute. I know in business we have a lot of numbers. WE have a lot of numbers that people want to see. We have a lot of charts. Numbers aren't really that exciting. I know that you know that. Numbers aren't really that exciting. How can we make them more interesting? I remember this teacher I had years ago, a long time ago, if college was 35 years ago, this was probably 40 years ago! She was an Algebra teacher and I wasn't crazy about Algebra, but , you know, I like comedy and all that and she was about as dry as you could possibly be. She got in there and everyday she'd go, good morning class and she'd go up to the board and start writing numbers again, again, again. I'm like ugh!!! This is going to be horrible. One day she came in and she came to the edge of the classroom and she said, "I have a joke for you!". Well I was like, I am all ears for this!!! An Algebra joke she says. I'm like, whatever. A joke about numbers. I'm still gonna listen. She says, "What is five Q plus five Q?". And we all said, "Ten Q!". And she said, "You're welcome." Well we all laughed! First of all, nobody expected it, which is one of the best things in your presentation. People aren't going to expect you to be that funny, but it was a cute joke and it lightened the mood and it helped us relate a little better.

Another one I want to talk about is another client that I had years ago. He had a bunch of numbers that he had to go over. He was a brilliant man! But his presentation was filled with mathematics including references to Descartes. I remember when he hired me he said I need you to do what you do. I said what's that and he said I need you to make me funnier, you know I have to be more entertaining, and I said okay. Let me take a look at what you got right now because I always take a look at video on the screen, you know take a look at what they look like on the screen and take a look and hear their content and everything like that. Well I watched this guy and I was, I don't know, about six minutes in and it was unbelievably dry, unbelievably dry! I don't want to say boring, but then I looked at how much video I had to go and it was like 55 minutes and I said I can't watch the whole thing. I immediately went to him and said we're going to have to change this. You're going to have to cut this in half, at least! We can't talk about numbers for fifty minutes, sixty minutes. It's not gonna work. People are gonna stop listening to you and that was back, this was like eight years ago, but even know we have less of an attention span as an audience, okay? So what I do is I try to find special talents of my clients and his special talent, cause he really wasn't that funny so it was tough to make him funny even reciting another joke. But what he could do is he could draw really, really well. I thought wow! And what he did was, and what he ended up doing is he drew funny pictures as he was giving his dry material. So once the audience caught on he would put his important points right in front of the drawing and as soon as he would end he would put the funny switch on the drawing! People were hanging on his every word because they laughed when they saw the drawing and listened to him. I thought what a great technique and you know that client ended up doing a TedX speech and I'm very, very proud of him. But that's TedX. Let's talk about that. It's the most successful business speaking venture of all time! And why? Because all of the videos are about eighteen minutes. They put a lot of time and research into this and they found out that eighteen minutes was about the attention span of what most people are going to give you in business to get your idea out and that's why they made it there.

Okay, so let's talk about the seven-minute presentation a little bit here. And I know you're thinking I gotta get all my stuff in there, but I gotta thank Alexis because the other day, probably two weeks ago, Alexis sent out an email and in that email it talked about the seven-minute Zoom presentation to the corporate partners. And in she put, all I want you to do is simply state who you are, what you do and how you're the best choice in your field. I'm like, woah, I love that! I love it when somebody does that! They tell us exactly, knowing what your audience wants. That's what we're doing. She tells us right now. All we got to do is let them know what we do, right? Who we are? And what makes us the best choice in the field. I love it!

And you know at the same time I got that email I got a call from a new client, a possible new client. We met a couple times, but they had won on Shark Tank. And they won on Shark Tank! And they called me and thought, huh, well that's interesting they already won on Shark Tank what do they need my services for, not that successful people don't hire me, but they already did a big time seven-minute presentation and got the deal on Shark Tank. So, I said I gotta find out how they won just like I do with every other client, I wanna watch the video. And I saw the video and you know what? They were extremely likeable! Now they had a great product, they had a great product like a lot of veteran owned businesses have great products., but they were extremely likable. They were just likeable on their own. Just naturally likeable and that's what really spurred on, I guess they had like three sharks fighting over them at one point. I did see that. But they were really likeable. So now we have that seven-minute presentation, let's be likeable! Because really we can't give anybody seven minutes on everything about the business, all the numbers or anything like that. Really what we want is we want that corporate partner to call us back. We want that connection. And That's what I do. I do short videos all the time.

I have this guy I know and I used to work with him a long time ago and he was so funny. He was a salesman, right? And he was a salesman at a dealership, and he did finance you know and the numbers were just, you know, so high! I can't believe he got anybody, but he was like the top salesman. But the problem was, when somebody objected, he got flustered and he would screw up the English language. Like he had one guy in his office who was just screaming at him and telling him, "I'm not signing this! You're ripping me off!" And he was like, "sir. Sir. Relax. You don't have to get ironic with me." The guy looked at him and said, "Ironic?! You mean Irate don't you?!"

He goes, "Yay, sir, it's okay. It's all right down here in black and blue." The guy started laughing again, but again he went black and blue? You mean black and white, don't ya?! Well the guy had such a good laugh and he sat down and just was telling him that, you know I just had a rough week, but I like you. I don't like the numbers, but you know what I'm gonna do? I'm gonna sign these papers because I like you. Now, isn't that it?! Eureka!! Right? Does anyone say Eureka anymore? No? Maybe it's just me. We found it, didn't we? We did! You have to be likeable because we all know, we're all in business here. Everybody on this call is in business and we all do business with people we like. Yeah! That's right! So in that seven minute presentation we're gonna tell them who we are, what we do and how we're the best choice in the field, but we're also going to be likeable because we all want that second call back. We all want to get into that room and meet them and then we can really shine! We can show them all the numbers and everything else that we have. And a lot of people go, "Dave, I know what you're saying, but I still have to show charts and graphs anyways." I'm like, Okay, okay, well make some of them funny once in a while, alright? You know, put a chart up there and show somebody without your product and, you know, maybe put a frown on their face. Show somebody holding your product with a smiley face on there, because it sends that message to them, right? That subliminal message and that's what we want to do.

Ok, so, what we're going to talk about now, we're going to talk a little bit about, I think we talked about Jesse a little bit, yeah. Same thing. A little bit of a water break here.

I like to do short videos myself too. I do short videos, you know, not seven minutes, but I do short videos because I want people to call me and contact me and contact me and that's what I do. I did a few months ago that I thought was really good and I got a few calls on it and I got some business and a friend of mine had commented on there, "Hey Dave! Great video, but no cats!". I was like no cats? What are you talking about? This is a business video. We don't have cats on video. He goes, but yeah everybody loves watching videos and they're watching cats on the video. Cats are really popular! And I mean I get it, cats are really popular and everything like that, but I mean so. And then I thought, you know what I'll do, how about if I put a blue bear? How about a blue bear? Are you guys...blue bear? I got the cow bell and a blue bear? Or how about this? This is a cat, it's a unicorn. People like David's unicorn. I can hold these up. I can be like when I make my point I can just bring these up (shakes silly bears and unicorns like a five year old!). How about like that? So it brings me to the point that people like cats and people like props you could work out, since people like props, how about let's have a little bit of fun, right? Uh, this is like my son's hat. This is something like you never see a bald guy wear. You never see a bald guy wear this cause he'll get scorched in there. But that's something you can do. Here you can use a heart. You can have fun with hearts, you know, I love NaVoba, right? I love the corporate partners, you know. I love the veteran owned businesses. Just a cute little thing like that, okay? Okay, here we go. How about this? Let's just show you, I want to show you my bear right here. I love this little guy. He's got a little lucky cloverleaf on him right there. And I got this for my son. I got him from one of those skill cranes. You guys ever try the skill cranes, you know at the bars and restaurants. You pay like a dollar and you get the crane and you go down (all arm motion of a crane). And I got this guy and it only took me like six hundred bucks to get it. So we're gonna keep it because..the skill crane..it's tough to deal with.

You can also do so, and I just want to give you some more ideas here. You can also do..how about this? How about a puppet, right? Right? How about we can do a puppet and you can use a puppet to make your point. (fumbles with puppet)

And I always think it's interesting how (still fumbling with puppet) I wanna see if I can figure it out here.. I'm not a puppeteer, but why not. We're going to use it today, right? So there ya go. You got a puppet right there. You can use a puppet to make your points, right? Sure! Let's see if I got a mask on me. Yeah I got a mask on here. Okay look, because we're all wearing masks these days and he doesn't need one because he's a puppet, but I need one. So as you put a puppet up like this (painfully fumbles, one handed with attempting to put a mask on!!!) and I hope you're getting ideas here. If you put a puppet up like this, see right here? (points to puppet) He can deliver any message you want to deliver to the corporate partners, anyway I got to put my mask on straight! Alright, never work with a puppet or a bald guy. Alright so you can do that, you know. Or you can give him a fake voice like,

"Hey you guys. Buy my product" (talking to puppet?)"

"Stop looking at me."

"You look familiar."

"What do you mean? It's probably because I bought you for my son. That's why I look familiar."

"No that's not it. That's not it."

"Well this is the end for you so you're almost done."

"Were you ever on the Muppets?"

"Oh get out of here"…(.manhandles puppet and puts him away)

"I got it! The Eagle!"

"No! No! That's not it."

Alright, so I'm just giving you ideas here because I want you to understand how important props can be to get our audience's attention because we got to remember ten to twelve hours a day of fatigue and you don't have to go crazy. You don't have to use the same props that I have. Smaller props work. Ideas work. You just have to remember that we want to get our audience's attention.

So I'm going to tell you a story about a guy that used to use props that I used to work with. His name was

T.C. Hatter. This guy was really good! He was a clown and he did a show, we used to open up for him, me and another guy, he did forty-five minutes in a comedy club without saying a word, just using nothing but props. And I thought, Wow! This guy's brilliant! He got laughs just as much as the comedian did and he did it without speaking and I thought, Man that's great!

I used to work with Howie Mandell once in a while. We did a show down at the I.C. Light amphitheater. Now I don't know if you've ever been to the I. C. Light Amphitheater, but it's a theater right by the river and there's train tracks in between. Now after I met Howie he realized that when one of the trains went by, they were really, really loud. Not your optimum conditions for doing a show as far as comedy because people have to hear you! Right? So he looked at me and he goes, "Hey man. He goes, these trains, they stop when we're doing the show?" and I'm like, "No, no. Every fifteen minutes buddy! So what he decided to do at that point was he had some props in his act, what he decided to do is because he didn't want to speak when the train was going by, but he did all of his props! I thought oh man that is really cool and the audience got it. They loved it when the train was going by. At that point I wish I had props in my act, but I didn't do it, but he was effectively delivering his message for the people that came to the show.

Okay, so now we're getting to, I think, what is one of the most important things about your audience. I think this is really the most important thing I can say is how your audience was conditioned to learn. I mean your audience conditioning to learn is so important and if you look back, everybody in our audience, two generations back now, was conditioned to learn through Edutainment. That's the combination of education and entertainment. So why is it so important? Look at all the shows. You know, Sesame Street, Mr. Rogers, there's Dora The Explorer, Syd the

Science kid. They have apps now that teach languages that make it fun, Duolingo. It's absolutely everywhere! So you have to try to incorporate some kind of humor, some kind of props, some kind of entertainment to deliver your message because your audience already conditioned to learn like that. Isn't that great!? So now that we know that our audience is already conditioned to learn like that all we have to do in our message is appeal to it. So now we know how our audience was conditioned to learn and how they want us to deliver their message to them, right? Well there's a guy, let me give you a really powerful example here before we move on to the quick coaching. There's a guy on CNBC named Jim Cramer and he talks about the stock market. That's his deal. That's his gig. You know he talks about the stock market and he sells stocks, but at the same time he has all kinds of props, bells, buzzers, whistles, lots of color and everything like that. And he's very successful at it. Well years ago when he first started his show, he did a live broadcast at Penn State University, This was probably two years after he's been on. A live broadcast at Penn State University's college campus. When he showed up thousands of kids showed up to watch his show. Thousands of kids! It's amazing! He did something really brilliant here. He used edutainment to make his show so popular that it actually appealed to college students from eighteen to twenty-two! What a brilliant move just by using edutainment. Now I don't know about you guys, but when I was in college I was not thinking about the stock market, nor was I fired up about it enough to show up to somebody speaking about it on a college campus. There were a lot of other things I was worried about. But he knew that people were already conditioned to learn like that so let me make my show be number one on CNBC so I'm going to use edutainment. Brilliant move!

Ok, that's all I have right there about humor and

everything like that. You can always contact me at Davidmichael@live.com and I'll be here to help you with any of your coaching needs.

Before I go here, I want to do some quick coaching things:

QUICK COACHING

Ok so now let's look at some things you can do right now....right this minute to immediately make you more effective. I like to call these techniques quick coaching because they will make an immediate impact. Remember that it's just small adjustments and less is more so quick coaching! Some seem like common sense, and they are, but when people are at home they get way too comfortable and forget they are still in business! My clients are surprised sometimes how much of a difference a few small adjustments can make.

1. Always dress professionally. Should I even be saying this? Unfortunately, yes. I can't tell you how many experienced businesspeople I have seen in ratty, relaxed clothes when speaking. Let's remember this is business and first impressions always mean something and, if you're lucky, a second impression can save you. I always dress professionally like I was in the same room with my clients because....I am. Just because you are at home or on the road doesn't mean you have to be relaxed. When you are dressed professionally you project a tone and the mindset that you are in charge and that this is important. Show you care enough to do so! Audiences in general

respect well-dressed speakers even before you say a word.

I had a relatively well-known influencer one time tell me that I needed his services. I certainly didn't think I did but I was willing to listen. I'm always willing to listen. He talked a big game and had all kinds of media and followers and told me how great he was and who he knew etc. So I agreed to do a video chat with him to find out how he could help me or actually how much he wanted me to pay. Well, we set the meeting up for early in the morning and as he greeted me, he was at his kitchen table in a t-shirt, unshaven, drinking a cup of coffee. He looked horrible. I mean really bad! I really couldn't believe it! Now I'm not sure what he was thinking but we are both in the same business of helping our clients be more successful, but this guy was asking for my business and future clients to boot! Needless to say, he didn't get my business and he lost every client I could have given him in the future. Not only is it disrespectful to show up on screen unprofessionally dressed but it has ramifications well beyond that meeting. For instance, ending up in my book as an example of the wrong thing to do! As we all know people talk! When you are well dressed, when you are on zoom, everyone notices, and it sets a precedent and an image of you being successful before you even get started. Isn't that what every speaker wants and needs before presenting? Yes!

2. Stand. Always stand when you are presenting on Zoom! Motion creates emotion and that's what you want! I always do a few

calisthenics or stretching exercises and try to get a good workout in before I present. It gets your blood pumping and keeps your mind working at a high level. We don't want to be stagnant or sluggish. Remember you are the show so let's take it to them! You want the audience to feel your energy and feed off it! Depending on your environment, you will need to prepare for this. Set your laptop or computer higher so the camera is eye level. This will allow you free range of motion and keep you moving and still keep you looking great on camera!

3. Smile and laugh. You knew this was coming ...right? I mean I'm a comedian! Of course, we are going to smile and laugh. Why? Say it with me here...Because audiences love and

respond to warm smiles and laughter is contagious! I think Tony Robbins did an experiment one time where he said if you get up in the morning and pretend you're in a good mood, you'll be in a good mood. If you smile and laugh eventually you will be in a good mood. You'll force yourself to be in a better mood. I know a lot of you aren't morning people, but if you're presenting in the morning, you'd better find a way to make it happen! People will enjoy your presentation more if they see you smiling and see you laugh at yourself and your mistakes. In short, this technique works so use it!

4. Cue cards. Always use cue cards. This is great because no one can see them! Nobody ever knows they are there, and they keep you centered on your presentation. This

accomplishes a couple of different needs. One, it makes you look like a pro as you don't have to continue to look down at a notebook or read off of 3 X 5 cards, remember the ones from junior high? You can have two easels, one on each side of your camera and as you go through your presentation your tech person or child volunteer can peel them off as you go along. You don't want to put your entire presentation on cue cards. You just want the topics and the main points listed underneath. You want to be able to just look at the subject and have it remind you of what you are going to say. This is also why I would never suggest to ever use a teleprompter. No audience member ever deserves to listen to someone read a presentation. It is stiff and the audience will be gone within minutes. The whole idea is to present! You are the show!

We just need something to remind us of the order of our presentation and a guide to come back to just in case something goes wrong, or we get sidetracked. If you prepare well, the outline and key points should be all you need to have on the cue cards. And it will happen so let's prepare for it!

5. Solid background. I always use a solid background. You want something that will allow your audience to focus on you. They already have enough distractions they certainly don't need any more ~ like your cat trying to eat your parakeet. Or your spouse coming through without pants on! Or your audience trying to read the books on your bookcase (which could be embarrassing) but not as embarrassing as losing the attention of the audience! Unless your background has to

be part of your presentation, maybe if you're an artist or cartoonist and have that as your background, you should stick with a solid color background. Try to keep it simple and always remember the ultimate goal of effectively delivering the message.

6. Prepare! Prepare! Prepare! This is just common sense but so true. Always prepare until you know your topic well. But also prepare for all the things that can go wrong. I know it's the comedian coming out of me again but, what I always train my clients to be prepared for the worst and when it happens, you're ready. When it happens, you can just smile and laugh and roll with it! One of the best ways to prepare is video yourself and maybe practice on Zoom with your tech person or a friend and then review your video and critique yourself. Not many people like this but it is necessary for your improvement. Video doesn't lie. It shows the good, the bad, and the ugly. The good news is you have time to correct any mistakes or bad habits you don't like. Have fun with it! Remember, you get to be the producer, the writer and the performer so take control of your presentation.

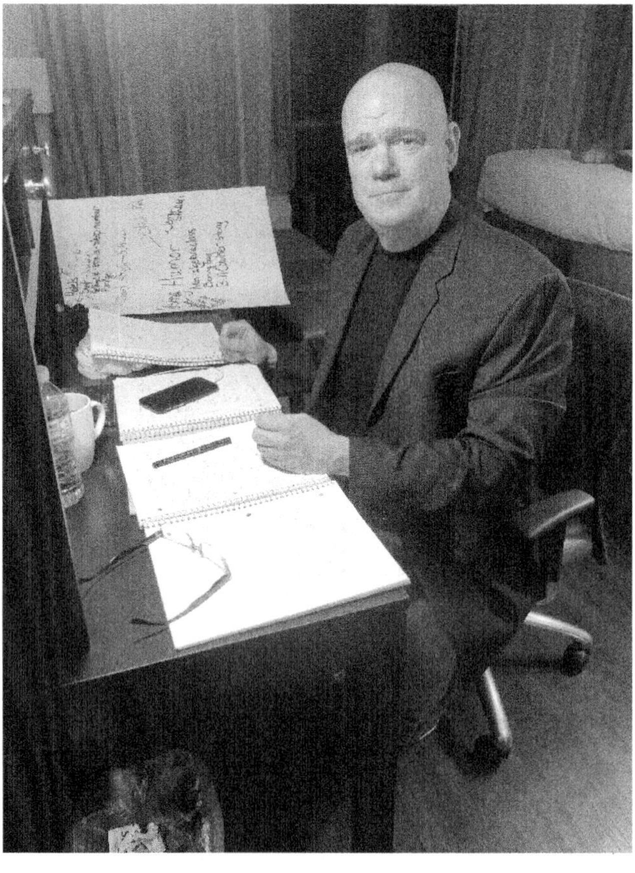

TECH STUFF

I can crush it on Zoom but I am really not good at technology. I mean that. When I work, I always have two others with me to make sure that when something goes wrong, I can have it covered no matter what. A tech person and an av person. The first reason is when something goes wrong, I want to be in front of the camera still talking and trying to engage the audience to keep their attention. Once you leave the view of the camera or step away from the presentation to do tech, sound, lighting, or video work the audience has a free get out of jail free card! They can go do whatever they want. And then when you get back, however long that may be, you have to find your audience again. Or what's worse is your audience seeing you fumbling with the camera and getting frustrated with the problem. Believe me it is a killer for your message and your presentation. Now, if you don't have a "team" or teens in your house who can help you, remember to use your humor and funny lines to handle this if it happens. Another advantage of having others there is for your sanity. It is difficult enough to present on Zoom without having the fear of something going wrong and you can't fix it! Remember as a comedian and speaker I always cover as many problems as I can before they happen because I know ...they are going to happen! This is another prep technique that will make u more

effective.

Now I understand that most don't have a team of people they can hire but I believe so strongly in this that you must at least try to have someone available that can troubleshoot and observe while you're presenting. A spouse, your teenager, a friend or maybe a local high school or college student looking to make a few dollars on the side. Believe me it is worth it. Zoom is not that difficult so you can learn a lot from videos, practicing and just experience. You can maybe grab a friend and together you can learn some of the basic knowledge. We are at the mercy of technology and anything can happen. Most of these things you can control, but some of them you can't. I am a big believer in Preparation! Preparation! Preparation!

One aspect about technology is we can do just about anything we want and look as smooth as possible. Backgrounds, intros, slides, vidoes, optical illusions, virtually everything you can imagine can be added to a presentation. There is one big drawback. While the tech can certainly highlight your better points and critical data, if you rely too heavily on it and it goes down, you could jeopardize your entire presentation. I would always make sure I can deliver my message without any help at all from the tech apps. That way if they go down or on the fritz you can still make light of it and continue your mission. Don't be held hostage by the technology and have your entire message depend on it working. Your message, and more importantly, your delivery has to stand on its own. The technology is there to enhance your message, not overpower it. I have seen too many speakers rely on their PowerPoint, pics, and videos and then have issues with them and their whole presentation is destroyed. Don't ever put yourself in that position. Remember we always want to have a backup plan for when things go wrong. So, create your message both ways and be ready to deliver both.

Another drawback is if you rely too heavily on tech and you're not speaking enough, you will lose the audience. As great as you may think all your highlights and achievements are, the audience may not enjoy your enthusiasm if you have to go to the video or PowerPoint too much. The audience's attention span is shorter than ever before and if they want to see pics and videos they will choose their own. As a presenter and speaker and as an entertainer you need to be the one running the show and that means speaking instead of simply showing content. If you have important videos or pictures to highlight your product or message, you can always direct your audience to hand outs, your website or even your book 😊 as a follow up after the presentation.

BRINGING IT ALL TOGETHER

I know these techniques and ideas seem foreign and sometimes overwhelming for a lot of folks, but the good news is you can start connecting on a higher level on Zoom with just small adjustments. Ideally, I would like you to start thinking of communicating before and during the writing of your presentation, but you can always add these powerful techniques to an already written speech or presentation, or as I like to refer to it, a performance. One of the things we do with our clients is help them incorporate humor and edutainment in their already prepared speech with small adjustments. Let's say you have an already prepared 20-minute presentation. I would typically add a little humor in the beginning of the presentation before you get into your topic. I would spend anywhere from 2 and 5 minutes on this. About 6 to 10 minutes into your presentation, I would add audience participation to make sure my audience is listening to the meat of my topic. Then about 15 minutes in I would use an example of edutainment, further strengthening my message for my audience. This would then segway into my close for an effective overall presentation. I would also consider a callback right after or near the closing comments. Remember my son and the Muppets comment from earlier in the book? Draw your audience back to that moment and tie it all together to them. Now that important point is connected to a funny story and they won't ever forget it. Now if your presentation is longer you can adjust the techniques and amount of time you spend on these three techniques, but we are still aiming for Less Is More!

Just these three adjustments placed strategically through your presentation will make your overall message more effective!

One of my favorite comedians, and a guy who puts all the techniques together, is Tim Cavanagh from Chicago. I've known Tim for about 30 years, and I can tell you he is one of the best when it comes to getting his audience to respond to him and hang on his every word. He is a former high school teacher who uses music and a very unique technique in getting his audience involved in his show and presentation. Tim certainly knows how his audience was conditioned to learn and Comedians all know that the quickest way to get your audience to like and listen to you is to break the fourth wall and get them involved. It is the same as speaking. Tim asks his audience to get involved right from the start urging his audience to reply to his questions with the phrase "Yeah Tim! Sounds like fun!" He then delivers his message by playing his guitar and singing it! As his performance moves forward the audience gets into it and hangs on his every word. Tim then has the advantage of taking his audience whenever he wants to go. That is exactly what you want when you speak. Finding a way to have interaction with your audience is a favorite technique of comedians and now speakers are increasingly using these techniques. Periodically involving your audience in your presentation greatly increases your odds of effectively communicating your message. Tim brilliantly uses the three major techniques in this book to effectively deliver his message every time he performs.

So on Zoom let's get our audience involved so they have to participate. Remember we most likely don't have the full attention of our audience and Zoom lets them off the hook by not being in the same room as we are. So we have to go for it and develop creative ways to get them to interact with us. We have to call them out! It sounds harsh, maybe, but if we are just speaking and the audience is just killing time doing other tasks during our presentation it is a total failure and everyone's time is wasted. So let's get creative and start to think like Tim does and have some fun with our audience. Maybe we can develop a quick game show with questions about our topic to our audience. Break up the audience into teams for a team building exercise and get them excited about participation. Maybe something as simple as asking the audience a few general questions about them, right up front, to get them used to paying attention and subtly letting them know you may be coming back and asking questions later in your presentation. Nobody wants to be embarrassed and caught off guard so if they think you're going to come back to them they have a greater incentive to pay attention!

WHY YOU NEED ME!

I would like to be your speaking coach! I want to make you a better speaker...a funnier and more entertaining speaker, but most of all I want to make you the most effective speaker you can be! The advantages to being the best communicator are endless when it comes to your career. Starting with more success, and always more money, but also gaining that satisfaction from the opportunities it will bring your way as well! I am dedicated to my clients and their success. It's important to me and I can get you there too!

A lot of people may wonder why anyone would need a speaking coach in business? I mean I wrote all this stuff down in this book for you, right? All you have to do is read it and you'll be good? Maybe, but remember, I focused on three of the top techniques for you to make an immediate impact. To be the best you have to continue learning, practicing and honing your skill. It isn't easy. I mean we all speak right? Some more than others and some better than others, but it's definitely something we all do. We all have delivered presentations, right? Well, there is a definite science and protocol to doing it effectively as we have seen in the book. There is a difference between just talking, just speaking, just delivering that speech, and effectively delivering that speech so it's understood, retained, remembered and enjoyed. But here is the real rub. I can't possibly give you everything I know in one book. Well, I could but it would be way too long and as we know, **Less Is More!** But there is so much more to know and learn! When I coach you and consult you on aspects of your presentation and delivery, you are actually getting all the experience I have from the last 35 years! I've done all the work for you. I've paid my dues on stage for you, learned from it, paid my dues again then perfected these techniques so you don't have to go through that! You're welcome!! I truly have seen it all in the business and entertainment industries. I have been on stage thousands of times and sometimes in the worst possible conditions. I have performed for every type of audience from small gatherings to sold out arenas and even prisons! Yes, prisons! When I say I've seen it and done it all, I really mean it! I have worked with the greatest comedians of the past generation! I have been in movies, television, radio, and have focused on the techniques that comedians use to effectively communicate their message for the past 35 years. I am an expert and the leader in this industry! I released my groundbreaking book, Secrets from the Greenroom a Comedians Inside Techniques to Effective Speaking, 10 years ago and I'm still going! These are simply the most powerful techniques you can use when speaking and I promise you I can deliver, and you will benefit from not only my coaching but my extensive experience with audiences. Repetition is the mother of skill and since you don't have 35 years to get on stage thousands of times, I'll teach you everything I know and you can always contact me anytime for any speaking needs you may have or coaching before, during, and after your presentation or event!

So, really, the decision is yours! But one final thing

on why you should consider a coach: Speaking is not easy!! As a matter of fact, it's hard...really, really hard for most people, but it is critical in business. Any sports fans here? Let's talk about sports. All the best athletes have several coaches. Look at golf. The best always have several coaches to get them to the top and keep them there. You can pick any of your favorite top athletes here but I'll use Tiger Woods. Golf is not easy. We all know way too well, don't we? Especially when we have to play in business outings! Tiger always has had a swing coach over the years. Now.Tiger has swung a club thousands of times since he was five years old. And yet he has invested lots of time and money in swing coaches over the years and is still doing it. Why? Because it's that important to his overall success. It's that important to keep going over and over and over it to make sure it's as perfect as it can be. Amazing right? The good news is I make it as easy as possible for you! We will write, choreograph, and direct your presentation so all you have to do is deliver it. It couldn't be any easier for you to start becoming a master communicator from the stage and screen. It is just another weapon in your arsenal and maybe the most powerful one in business. I believe it is the most important factor in business for leaders and ultimate success. So contact me right now and let's CRUSH IT!

For More information about David

Contact

davidmichael@live.com

CRUSHitonZOOM.com

Printed in Great Britain
by Amazon